What Does My Dream Mean?

What Does My Dream Mean?

Interpret Your Dreams Today

Theresa Sullivan & Instafo

instafo

ISBN 978-1-974-45189-0

Printed in the United States of America

First Edition

CONTENTS

What Does My Dream Mean?

Chapter 1:

Awaken Yourself to Your Dreams

It Was Just a Dream, or Was It?

"A dream which is not interpreted is like a letter which is not read."

- Extracted from the Talmud

(a central text of Rabbinic Judaism)

Nothing is more wonderful than waking up one morning wishing you could go right back to sleep to continue a wonderful dream. Most of us have enjoyed this pleasant experience at least once in our lives.

On the other hand, dreams also have the power to terrify us - waking us up with a pounding heart and a gasping breath.

Whether your dreams are run-of-the-mill or bizarre, delightful or frightful, trivial or significant, you have probably been curious to learn the meaning behind these incredible subconscious experiences.

Dreams often occur following a shocking event or when we have an urgent, unfulfilled desire (perhaps a new love interest or a pending business idea). This is because our dreams are reflective of our feelings at any particular point in time. When our emotions are heightened, they are often reflected in our dreams.

Searching for Answers? Look to Your Dreams

Knowing how to correctly interpret your dreams is incredibly beneficial in managing your daily life and making choices. How many of us, when faced with a difficult decision, are given the wise advice, *"Why don't you sleep on it first?"*

"Sleeping on it" makes perfect sense considering the following:

- Dreams help you understand your current state of mind. Our mind registers our emotions and regulates our sensitivity to the world. Once we are marked negatively or positively by something, our mind reacts accordingly.

- Dreams reveal how recent events have affected you. You may convince yourself a situation is no big deal, while in reality it has deeply affected you. Often these repressed emotions will manifest as a series of odd dreams.

- Dreams might possibly be reminding you of something you may have forgotten. As strange as it seems, it is not uncommon for an old memory or event to come back to you in your dreams.

- Dreams might reveal events that are to come. This is the case in premonitory dreams, where your dreams act as a warning about something that will happen soon.

From the Man Himself - The Father of Psychoanalysis

Of course, no discussion on the human mind would be complete without mentioning Sigmund Freud, the 20th-century German psychologist also known as the father of **Psychoanalysis.**

In his book, *The Interpretation of Dreams,* Freud said:

> "Properly speaking, the unconscious is the real psychic; its inner nature is just as unknown to us as the reality of the external world, and it is just as imperfectly reported to us through the data of consciousness as is the

> external world through the indications of our sensory organs."

There is no doubt that our dreams can tell us a lot about ourselves. However, here Freud is telling us that our dreams are even more powerful than we could ever imagine; they literally have psychic powers! And while the inner nature of the subconscious is still quite mysterious to us, the information we receive through our dreams can be more revealing than the information we receive while we are awake.

This guide will teach you four methods for deciphering your dreams with the intent to increase your self-awareness and possibly even unlock the mysteries lurking in your subconscious.

Chapter 2:

Crack the Code of "Symbolism"

The Expression of the Subconscious

Paying close attention to the **symbolism** within a dream is a highly effective technique for interpretation. This is because the dreaming mind has a unique way of revealing our innermost thoughts.

Symbols can help us recognize our obsessions, clarify our goals, or refocus our attention. For example, a student hard at work at school may dream of graduation day. This dream may refocus the student's attention on obtaining their goal.

Let's look at a more detailed example of symbolism:

> Imagine a young girl who wants the latest Barbie doll. She sees the commercial on Nickelodeon every day and can't wait for her mother to buy it for her. Her desire is so strong that she has pleasant dreams about the doll. Sometimes she dreams of holding the doll in her hands and other times she sees a beautiful blonde woman with pink high heels, and a pink outfit.

Now, how would you interpret such a dream?

1.) Always start by noting the person's state of mind before the dream. In this case, we know that this little girl is obsessed with the doll.

2.) Look for any symbols that appear within the dream, particularly if they are recurrent. The little girl she sees the doll (the object of desire), but she also dreams of the doll as a human being. This may show that the child wishes she was a Barbie doll herself.

3.) Consider the foretelling message behind the dream. You could conclude that this little girl may grow up to become a beauty queen since she is captivated by pretty dolls from an early age.

Do you see how symbolism can reveal a lot about the dreamer?

Here we could analyze the little girl's state of mind (she is obsessed with the doll) and gain a glimpse at the type of person she may become in the future (possibly a beauty queen).

TIP: Get a **dream journal**; and the moment you wake up, immediately jolt down your dream while it is still fresh in your mind, otherwise you'll forget it or not remember it as vividly as you fall back asleep and wake up again or as the day progresses

How Symbolism Works

To put symbolism to work for your own dream interpretation, follow these steps:

STEP 1: Take note of the symbols that you remember from your dream. Include as many details as possible by noting specific places (like a church, a school, the woods, etc.) and including details like color (like the color of an outfit) and any feelings associated with the symbol (happiness, fear, anger, etc.).

STEP 2: Hypothesize their meaning: for instance, white represents purity, something untouched, something that is clean, etc. If there are several possibilities, note all that come to mind.

STEP 3: Put together a list of events that you think could be attached to each detail. Let's say with white you can correlate this with marriage, new resolutions, etc.

STEP 4: Draw connections represented in the dream, by asking questions such as:

- **What does this color mean when it is present in this venue/place?** If you dream of wearing white in a church, there might be a wedding happening soon.

- **What does the symbol represent when it elicits a certain emotion?** If you dream of a snake biting you and you are frightened, the snake may represent an adversary. Take all possibilities into consideration.

- **What do objects or people from my past mean about my life in the present?** It is quite common to dream of things from our childhood. This could translate into a desire to be close to a lost loved one, or to organize a family get-together.

In this step of the interpretation, you can see that we've used symbolic details within a dream to draw possible conclusions. Some may be obvious, but others will be much more difficult. The mind has its own language, rich in symbolism, which means it may take some work to find the meaning.

STEP 5: Draw your conclusion. What was the purpose of the dream?

What Is It Trying to Tell You?

Let's now use an example to better illustrate this technique:

Imagine that you dream of a giant lizard attacking you and biting your neck. While you can feel its claws and teeth on your neck, you are helpless to stop the attack.

To interpret this dream, follow these steps:

STEP 1: Recognize the symbolism in your dream and your feelings. In this case, the lizard is the symbol, and your fear and helplessness are the feelings.

STEP 2: Determine the meaning behind the symbol. The reptile/creature represents adversity.

STEP 3: Draw a list of possible events that could be attached to the symbol. Relax and think about a possible connection to a hardship you've *recently* faced - perhaps an argument you've had with somebody. Keep in mind that the connection may not be obvious at first. Remember that sometimes we underestimate the impact an event has had on us. Our subconscious is often more sensitive to issues that arise in our daily lives.

STEP 4: Draw your conclusion. The dream was a warning for you to resolve the conflict before the issue escalates.

Exercise: Decode Your Recent Dream

Before we move on, do the following exercise:

1.) Considering a recent dream, take note of the symbols that you can remember.

2.) Determine the meaning behind each symbol.

3.) Draw a list of events that you think could be associated with the symbol.

4.) Match the symbol with the places represented in the dream *(if necessary)*.

5.) Draw your conclusion.

Examples:

Dream 1: You are in a garden surrounded by water. There is a child playing and enjoying the garden. The child turns and runs to you with a smile, calling you mommy/daddy.

Dream 2: You are in a church, dressed in white, surrounded by everyone you have ever known.

Chapter 3:

Connect the Dots with "Parallelism"

The Translation of Your Feelings

"Dreams are illustrations... from the book your soul is writing about you."

- Marsha Norman

(American playwright, screenwriter, novelist, and receiver of the Pulitzer Prize for drama)

Some dreams have less to do with specific symbols and more to do with recent events that trigger a strong **emotional response**. When a significant event is experienced, our dreams tend to reflect our emotions.

To interpret these dreams, you must compare the details of the dream to recent events that prompted an emotional response such as fear, anxiety, anger, joy, etc. This is done through **parallelism.**

By connecting the details of a dream with a recent event, you'll gain clarity on how to respond to a certain situation, whether that is seeking help or simply laying the issue to rest.

How Parallelism Works

This is how interpretation by parallelism works:

STEP 1: As you wake up from a dream, you should quickly note the scenes that impacted you the most in your dream journal.

STEP 2: Spend 20 more minutes noting every detail you can. Close your eyes, relax and write down as much as you can remember, even if it just a few details.

STEP 3: Make a list of recent noteworthy events in your life going back about two weeks. Start your list with a date, include the location and names of the people involved, and a description of the situation. Example: *"Monday at 9 AM I had a terrible stomach ache after drinking some exotic coffee. Tuesday at 3 PM my boss asked that I review the coffee, etc."*

STEP 4: Compile the information you've gathered by listing the **details of your life** on the left side of the page and the **details of the dream** on the right side of the page. You will obviously end up with more details of your life over two weeks.

STEP 5: Begin eliminating the **details on the left side** (life events) that *don't correlate* with the **details on the right** (information from your dream).

STEP 6: Eventually, you will end up with a concise list of life events that precipitated your dream. Take a close look at these events and evaluate the impact they have on your mind. *Are you feeling afraid, angry, excited or hopeful?* You should have a greater awareness of your emotions and how you should effectively respond.

As an example, you dream about fighting with someone.

When listing your recent life events, you note that you set a personal goal a few weeks ago that is giving you some anxiety. By using the technique described above, you will match the fight with your anxiety stemming from the pursuit of your goal.

You can then conclude that you are doubting yourself because of your difficulty following through on your goal. The fight represents your struggle in achieving your goal.

After your conclusion is drawn, you can find a solution for your anxiety. Perhaps you need to work harder or make some smaller, more attainable goals.

Exercise: Decipher Feeling About Recent Events

Before moving on to the next dream interpretation method, here's an assignment for you to put this to the test.

Use one of your recent dreams to do the following:

1.) Note the scenes that have influenced you the most while you were dreaming.

2.) Spend 20 minutes remembering and noting additional details.

3.) Draw a list of significant events in your daily life, going back two weeks in time.

4.) Compile your lists and eliminate the details that don't match the details of your dream.

5.) Evaluate the remaining life events and how they have impacted you: *are you scared or excited, unhappy or happy about something?* Draw your own conclusion and then come up with a plan to respond.

Chapter 4:

Uncover New Knowledge in "False Awakening"

The Pending Solutions to Problems

"All the things one has forgotten scream for help in dreams."

- Elias Canetti

(Language author, playwright, and non-fiction writer)

Have you ever woken up from a dream in a *bewildered* state? You didn't even realize you were dreaming as every experience felt so real.

These dreams are called "**false awakening dreams**," and they often occur when you've been engrossed in a problem or project prior to falling asleep.

Your brain will actually continue working while you are asleep. You awake knowing that you've experienced something remarkable and you are desperate to put the pieces together and make sense of it all.

Physiologists Eugene Aserinsky and Nathaniel Kleitman from University of Chicago were pioneers in sleep research who discovered that dreaming takes place during **REM** (rapid eye movement) sleep.

This demonstrated that even at rest, the brain was still active during certain sleep cycles.

Note that these dreams will have clear messages as opposed to coded messages. A clear message is revealed through simple scenes, where there are no odd symbols or creatures, while coded messages often come in sequels, and have animals and symbols.

Planting a Seed

Let's say your brain had an overly active night solving problems and you want to tap into this new knowledge. *What are you to do?*

To make sense of your dream, follow this method:

STEP 1: Start by breathing in and out slowly and deeply to relax your mind and boost your concentration.

STEP 2: Slowly replay your dream in your mind, taking notes on as many details as possible.

STEP 3: Make sure you go slowly and open your eyes widely as if the dream was unveiled in front of your eyes.

STEP 4: Continue until you have replayed the last scene you can remember.

STEP 5: Interpret *(read)* the message behind the dream.

Realities within Dreams

Let's go through a few examples to illustrate working with false awakening dreams.

CASE 1: Adam was studying for his accounting course all night. In the past few weeks he had avoided studying, and now he was devoting all his energy to it in an attempt to pass the course. After practicing 10 exercises, he went to bed at around 3 AM, without completing the 11th exercise. A few minutes into his sleep, he sees the rest of exercise 11 unveiling right in front of his eyes (while still dreaming). The next morning when he wakes up, he can't believe what he saw in his dream.

CASE 2: Dina will be giving an important presentation that demands a lot of research and a complete understanding of her company's policies. Although she is incredibly anxious the night before, the last thing she thinks about before going to bed that night is to stay calm and everything will be alright. While sleeping, she sees herself on a beach smiling, eating seafood, and with a cocktail in her hand. She looks stunning in a beautiful bathing suit and everyone is smiling at her. A handsome man invites her to swim with him in the ocean. The dream ends when she reaches the water with the man. The last scene from her dream is the handsome fellow smiling at her. The next day, she wakes up in a great mood. She's enthusiastic and optimistic that it will be a successful presentation.

How should Adam and Dina effectively interpret all this?

Case 1 - Adam's Dream:

STEP 1: Adam takes slow, deep breaths to increase his concentration.

STEP 2: He replays his dream in his mind while taking notes. For example, he sees a balance sheet with assets listed to the left and liabilities on the right.

STEP 3: He opens his eyes wide, as if the dream were being unveiled before his eyes and slowly goes through the scenes of his dream. He now sees numbers adding up and being put in the right accounts.

STEP 4: Adam carries on until he replays the last scene of his dream. Through relaxation, he allows himself to remember other specific details, while recording them on a piece of paper. For instance, the totals for liabilities and assets match one another.

STEP 5: The last step would be for him to interpret *(read)* what his dream reveals. Adam's brain was still working on the final exercise while he was asleep, which led him to a new interpretation. Now he can attempt exercise 11 again, this time with the new perspective provided by his dream.

Case 2 - Dina's Dream:

STEP 1: Dina begins by breathing in and out, boosting her concentration.

STEP 2: She slowly replays her dream in her mind while taking notes on a piece of paper. She sees herself smiling, eating delicious food and drinking a cocktail as if she doesn't have a care in the world.

STEP 3: Going slowly, she opens her eyes wide as if the dream were being unveiled before her eyes. By replaying it calmly, she can relive the scenes of the dream as if she were still dreaming.

STEP 4: She continues until she has replayed the dream in its entirety.

STEP 5: Finally, she can interpret *(read)* what her dream is revealing to her. The dream is showing her greatest fantasy: a relaxing beach trip where she feels and looks amazing, while eating delicious food, and enjoying the company of a handsome man. The scene is peaceful and Dina feels confident and in control. She realizes she needs to calm herself, refocus, and carry on with her presentation. Dina knows good things come to those who are calm and in control of the situations that they face *(even the unpredictable ones)*.

Remember, the next time you are working on an important project, whether as a student or a professional, pay close attention to your dreams! The information gained from your subconscious may be just what you need to ensure your success.

Exercise: Make Sense of False Awakening

Now it's time for you to get a better sense of false awakening dreams.

1.) Go through the scenarios below and **match them** with the corresponding dream.

2.) Draw your own conclusion for each dream.

3.) Keep in mind that there are no right or wrong answers. The goal is to practice dream interpretation from your own perspective.

(Don't hesitate to do some research if a name is unfamiliar to you. It will only take a few seconds.)

Pre-Dream Scenarios:

- This wishful thinker works very hard and wishes he/she had a break with the children.
- This romanticist recently discovered Rachmaninov's work on YouTube.
- This brainstormer is struggling with a theme for his/her next project.

Dream Details:

- Desiree dreams about a piano teacher instructing her how to play the piano. The teacher moves Desiree's hands around the keys and she can feel his breath on her skin.
- Collin dreams of an interview on CNN, where he is presented as the next up-and-coming writer. He

reveals a book title and is questioned about a particular chapter of the book.

- Saskia dreams about taking her kids to the pool, where they are attended by maids who treat them with milkshakes and cake.

Chapter 5:

Discover Inspiration through "Reenactment"

The Inception of Inspiration

"Dreams are more real than reality itself, they're closer to the self."

- Gao Xingjian

(Chinese novelist, playwright, and 2000 Nobel Prize winner)

Major dreams often occur when our routines are *disrupted.*

For the most part, our lives are made up of routines that become comfortable over extended periods of time. When these patterns are disrupted, dreams are likely to occur. Alternatively, routines can become so repetitive that the mind fixates on them, stimulating dreaming.

That's why dream interpretation is such a valuable asset. It gives you insight into your state of mind at the time, and can lead you to make life-altering changes to your daily routines.

It is important to proceed with this process in a structured manner to avoid confusion and ensure you get the best possible result.

STEP 1: Replay the dream in your mind and write down whatever you can remember about the dream. It does not need to be in chronological order.

STEP 2: Note which scenes carry great significance, which we will call "**peak periods**" of the dream. They can be scenes that felt as if they lasted a long time or scenes where something strange or unusual happened. Highlight or mark these scenes as *significant*.

STEP 3: Order the events of your dream with a **vague/non-important scene** followed with a **peak scene.** Vague scenes are the scenes that you can barely remember that often appear blurry in your dream. So, it should be one **vague scene** followed by a **peak scene**, one **vague scene** followed by a **peak scene**, and so on.

STEP 4: Reenact the dream by physically doing every movement, and noticing every detail as if you were in the dream. If necessary, repeat the simulation three more times, making sure that you have all the pieces of the dream together. You'll notice that this reenactment will reveal the emotions that are triggering your dreams.

STEP 5: Make your own conclusions of the dream.

The Reenactment of a Dream

Let's now go through an example to demonstrate this:

> Jocelyn lives in Manhattan and works for a recruiting agency. For several weeks now, she has dreamt about walking down the same path to the subway station that she takes every morning. She is concerned about this recurring dream, and wonders what it means.

Now, what does this dream reveal about Jocelyn? Let's follow the steps to find out:

> STEP 1: She begins by writing down what she remembers about the dream: places, colors, gestures, possible people, sounds, and any other recollection.

> STEP 2: On the list, she notes the peak periods of her dream. For example, she should note what happens in the dream once she reaches the subway: *Is this scene the*

same every time she has this dream? Are there new details coming into play? Is this scene the longest?

STEP 3: Order the dream with a vague/non-important scene followed by a peak scene. She should put the scene where she crosses the street first, followed by the one where she is at the subway. Vague scenes should be followed by clearer scenes.

STEP 4: Jocelyn will next reenact the scenes she wrote down in the order she put them in during STEP 3. So, she will cross the street, walk down the stairs, and wait for the train that takes her to work. It's important for her to pay attention to each detail she pulled from the dream. Doing this process should reveal the true emotions behind her recurring dreams. For example, she may be disgusted by the condition of the subway and feel sorry for herself that she has to ride it every day.

STEP 5: She then draws her own conclusion. Which may be that she is exhausted by her daily routine and craves a change of some sort.

STEP 6: Finally, she must find a solution. *What is she going to do about her revelation?* She could do something drastic like quitting her job and moving to another country or she could simply change one detail of her routine to make it less repetitive. For instance, on Wednesday and Fridays, she could treat herself to a latte or cappuccino, or she could get off the subway a stop earlier and enjoy a leisure walk to work.

Exercise: Understand the Next Path to Follow

Read the previous example one more time, then try going through the interpretation phases with these examples below as exercises.

Make sure you follow each step thoroughly and come up with your conclusions and solutions for each dream.

Dream 1: Mackenzie went to the zoo for the first time and saw an elephant. She was so amazed that she had several dreams where she is in a tropical jungle looking for elephants.

Dream 2: Steven had a dream about driving the latest Ferrari that he had seen earlier on a TV commercial.

Chapter 6:

Interpret Dreams Using Different Methods

Dream 1: Dream-Teller Interpretation

Tommy has been having recurring dreams of flying above a mountain of pastries and vegetables. He had just started a diet and fitness program two weeks ago.

Which technique do you think he should use to interpret this dream successfully: the symbolism technique or the parallelism technique? Or should he replay or reenact his dreams to find answers?

Dream 2: Symbolism Interpretation

Jada has been having the same dream every week, where she sees herself playing with a newborn baby in the most luxurious nursery imaginable.

Use the symbolism technique to interpret this dream, then form a conclusion and possible solutions to her issue *(if you believe she has one)*.

Dream 3: Parallelism Interpretation

Using Jada's dream from exercise 2, apply the guidelines for the parallelism technique.

To help you match Jada's reality with the scenes from the dream, here is some information on what has been going on in her life the past two weeks:

She has been feeling sick every morning, with pain in her stomach.

Dream 4: Reenactment Interpretation

Steven is tired of having his mother-in-law in his business all the time. Lately, he's been having dreams about being in a peaceful place, lying down in a bright room with white linen sheets.

What should Steven do to interpret this dream? Write out guidelines for him to follow to reenact his dream. Come up with three possible conclusions and three solutions to his problem.

Chapter 7:

Let Your Dreams Set Sail

Thoughts Revisited

Mankind stands apart from the rest of creation because of the remarkable, highly-functioning human brain. Every day, our brains process massive amounts of information and control our emotional responses.

As we mature, most us of us learn to keep our emotions in check during our waking hours; however, these emotions will often reveal themselves through our dreams. This is why, depending on our mental state, dreams can be anything from awe-inspiring to disturbing.

As William Dement, a pioneering American sleep researcher and founder of the Sleep Research Center at Stanford University put it, *"Dreaming permits each and every one of us to be quietly and safely insane every night of our lives."*

This statement beautifully illustrates the power of our dreams, with their mysterious symbols, and messages. Tapping into this power through dream interpretation means that you can process your emotions more effectively, uncover your deepest desires and maybe even foretell future events!

Sweet Dreams

We have provided you with several dream interpretation techniques to successfully decode symbolism, make connections with your life experiences, uncover new knowledge, and provide insight into your state of mind.

Ultimately, this will lead you to effectively solve your problems and lead a more fulfilling life.

So tonight, jump into bed, throw on your eye mask and dream on with your dream journal right by your side!

You are ready to interpret your dreams like a pro dream master.

14724618R00032

Printed in Great Britain
by Amazon